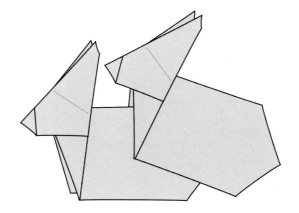

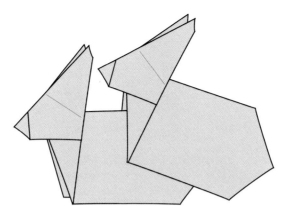

VERY NAUGHTY ORIGAMi

Nick Robinson

universe

Contents

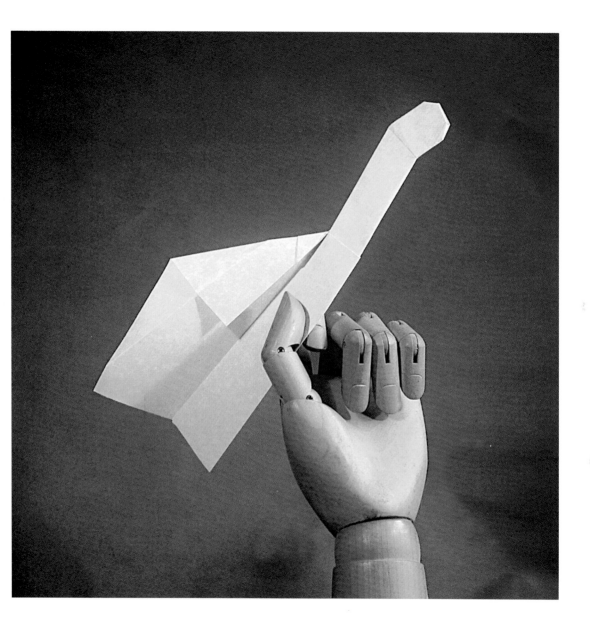

Introduction

WHAT IS NAUGHTY ORIGAMI?

"Origami" is formed from two Japanese words: "ori" (to fold) and "gami" (paper). It has a long and fascinating history, far beyond the scope of this book.

As with any creative art form, origami has many different approaches and styles. Naughty Origami is an obscure but important strand of origami, where the paper is folded into erotic toys, stylised representations of sexual activity, or knobs and pussies.

Many practitioners of conventional origami are unaware of this little-known facet of their art. Other, less liberally-minded folders are offended by it and feel there is no place for origami cocks and rubbers at the dinner table. However, the cultured paper-folder will find the style and content of Naughty Origami fascinating and may well begin to dabble creatively in the area.

It has often been argued that conventional origami is merely a development of Naughty Origami and that you can trace the roots of most modern designs to a naughty counterpart from many centuries ago. Indeed, even the language of modern origami contains subtle clues. If you take a peek inside any origami book, you will find a range of suggestive terms, such as "climactic fold", "sink inside", "swivel" and "reverse behind". Some designs require you to put your mouth to a hole. Others involve a repeated gentle pulling action. I rest my case.

When you've lost your marbles...

A BRIEF HISTORY

While now recognized as a truly international pastime, Naughty Origami has its roots firmly planted in Japan. Using archives discovered in very old caves, along with folklore, carbon dating and idle gossip, it has been possible to present— for the first time ever—an accurate time-line of this fascinating hobby, stretching from the very earliest times to the modern day.

YOMON PERIOD CA 11,000–CA 250BC

According to archaeologists, the earliest settlers in Japan were a tribal people called the Ainu. Leaves from the local mulberry trees provided for their toiletary needs, but were exceedingly rough to the touch. This rapidly led to the development of paper as we know it. They still had no knowledge of origami, but knew all about sex. The future of the Japanese population was assured.

TOFU PERIOD CA 250BC–552

The Tofu period is also called the Tumescent Period. "Tumesce" is the Japanese word for a typical kind of soft clay sculpture, often that of a phallus or sheep. Monks began to create simple folded shapes, which were both offered up as tributes to the gods and used at ceremonies such as births and same-sex weddings.

YOSUKA PERIOD 552–794

At the start of the Yosuka Period, the Milsanbuhn culture and thinking spread from China into Japan. The beginnings of Naughty Origami can also be traced to this time, when carefully-folded paper condoms were regularly used. This origami discipline gradually developed its own unique set of rules and strictures, known as the art of kokigami.

In search of nirvana.

Heyjo Period 794–1185

During this period a more distinctive Japanese erotic art culture began to develop. In the year 1001 we have hand-written records relating the torrid tale of the Lady Muramic Shikibu-ti, a servant to the Empress Akiki-kuki, who herself wrote the story of "Evil Monogamari", a travelling magician who used Naughty Origami to entice young women into his dressing room, to slake his wicked lust thereupon.

Kamakame-Lion Period 1185–1333

In 1180 a fierce war broke out between the ruling clans of the Heilo-moto and the Tara-chuk, both of whom were striving to capture the Naughty Origami diagrams of the other. Ownership of these sacred instructions was considered to give everlasting happiness. The blood of many generations was spilt before they decided to make copies and share them.

Muromachi Period 1333–1573

This is also known as the Ashe-tofpaipa Period after the clan that took control of the country. Zen Buddhism became more popular in Japan and influenced Japanese erotic art with such spiritual guidance as, "I fold, therefore I eat," and, "A foolish man folds underwater".

Edo Period 1603–1868

The Edo Period is named after the number of foreign folders or "gaijin" who began to visit Japan in search for erotic designs. They would enquire of the local populace, "I say, you there, who makes Naughty Origami masterpieces hereabouts?" to which he would receive the answer, "Edo", accompanied by a pointing thumb. One of the major artistic achievements of the Edo Period were uya-babi kmonnau folds, created by the master folder Pan-te-Nuido. He was the first folder to attempt to capture the sounds of lovemaking in a sheet of paper.

Mingin Period 1868 Onwards

By the end of the 19th century, almost all the traditional forms had been stolen by unscrupulous Western authors. For this, many fell victim to an ancient Japanese curse whilst others moved into tabloid journalism. This led the Japanese to start a campaign to acquire Western skills in all fields of high culture, including the erotic arts. Today, Japanese practitioners can produce Naughty Origami of the most accurate kind, such as that by "two testicles" Kir Chen Baum, the first origamist to achieve the impossible feat of folding a phallus, including both balls and a hand to hold it, from a single sheet of paper.

A Geisha perfects her oral technique whilst fending off an admirer.

TECHNIQUES YOU'LL NEED

Paper-folding diagrams for any type of origami use a standard set of symbols that allow people to follow instructions, even in another language. Here are the basic symbols you will need for this book:

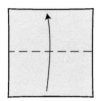

Valley fold—the paper is folded upwards. You can make this fold with the paper flat on the table.

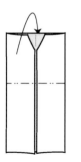

Mountain fold—the paper is folded downwards. You do this "in the air" (i.e. off the table) or turn the paper over and fold as for a Valley fold.

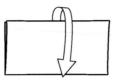

Pull the paper out—there are often hidden flaps, which may need to be pulled out gently. It may also be used to mean unfold the last few steps.

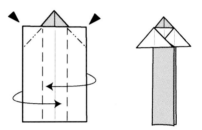

Apply gentle pressure—as you complete some moves, the paper flattens into a new position. The arrow indicates the general direction of pressure.

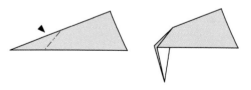

Reverse fold—precrease (fold, then unfold) then push the paper inside so that longest edge reverses direction.

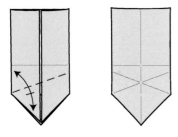

Fold and unfold—various arrows indicate where to fold to and then unfold.

Repeat—a fold arrow with a small dash across it means a move must be repeated, usually on the other side of the paper.

Existing crease—when you have unfolded a flap, you'll see a thin crease line. This is often used to locate another fold.

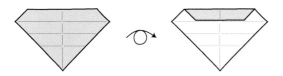

Turn the paper over—toss the sheet over, as it were.

TIPS FOR FOLDING

- Always fold with clean hands on a flat surface, such as a table or a firm bed. With some climactic folds, clean your hands after folding as well.
- Fold in silence, free from disturbances.
- Don't try to brush your teeth at the same time.
- Check the next step so you can see how it's supposed to look, even if you've absolutely no idea how to get there.
- Read the words too. They can help a lot.
- Make each design three times before moving on. Each will be much better than the last and this process will also help you memorize the sequence.
- Be creative. Alter angles and lengths to suit your own personal requirements.
- Prepare your Naughty Origami prior to commencing sexual relations—you'll find it difficult to fold neatly during foreplay.
- Practise folding in the dark: it will undoubtedly assist you in putting on a condom.
- If you simply cannot finish a design, send a blank check to the author, who will almost certainly help you out.

Mons

The mons, or *Mons veneris* to use its proper name, is Latin for "Mound of Venus". The exquisite geometry of this most fundamental part of the female form has fascinated artists, most men and some women since the dawn of time. Even schoolboys know how to draw one, although they may be less familiar with the mechanics.

The male organ is generally on display, with some men more often than others. Usually a pair of tight trousers shout, "Look at me!" to anyone who might be interested. The female equivalent, by comparison, hides its mysteries within. Even the tightest pair of panties reveals little unless you're adept at lip-reading. Compared with the frankly unappealing sight of a flaccid male organ, the aesthetic appeal of this object of desire lies in the simplicity and mystery, linked to the duality of pleasure and procreation that it represents. Probably.

Whilst the guidebook for arousing the male organ is fairly concise ("rub it"), the process for "turning on" women requires somewhat more effort and concentration.

This design by Japanese master Kunihiko Kasahara exemplifies the Zen approach to Naughty Origami, that of "more is less". Indeed, his original concept didn't even include the folds in Step 1. These days, we are starting to rediscover the joys of a more rounded curve to the hips.

With a few gentle and carefully placed creases, we can recreate the wonder that is the mons. You can fold this from a square or a rectangle, which will produce a taller, more elegant form. As you carefully press the paper to create the V-shape (Step 3), become one with the paper, feel in your heart it is the real thing you are touching. Become at one with the mons.

I'm guessing more men than women will fold this design, but that could just be symbolic of how unreconstructed my attitude towards genitalia is. In either case, it is essential that you fold with feeling.

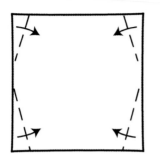

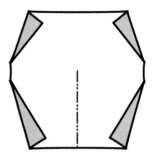

1. Start with a square or rectangle of paper with the shorter edge towards you. Fold in the four corners to produce the shape of the hips.

2. Make a mountain fold which roughly extends to the center of the paper, by folding either side to meet underneath.

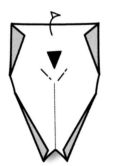

3. Holding the two sides together, carefully and gently press the end of the crease down slightly. This will produce two new creases pointing roughly towards the corners of the paper.

4. Turn over and let the paper unfold slightly.

An eager reader of Naughty Origami.

Schwanstucker

What can you say about this relatively small but highly significant part of the male anatomy? Apart from snide remarks about it being where men keep their brains, perhaps the most important aspect from the male perspective is size. Measurement and comparison play a vital part in the a teenage male's development, and penis-mythology is rampant in the schoolyard.

So what are the facts? The smallest penis measures slightly less than $\frac{1}{5}$ inch when erect and is known as a "micropenis". Leaving aside genetic mutations, the largest male organs clock in at around 11 inches. Any larger than that and it's a medical fact that men would faint whenever they had an erection. In any case, whilst monster organs (and I don't mean the Hammond L100) might impress fellow users of the men's room, it's most likely to frighten most women half to death.

Men do like to personalize their penis, indeed to treat it as a close friend. Many share the name "John Thomas" or "Percy". Other terms include pecker, dick, cock, pocket python, dong, giggle stick, knob, one-eyed trouser snake, pecker, peter, pool cue, pud, schlong, schwanz, skin flute, tallywhacker, wanger, rumpleforeskin, tadger, pork sausage, pink oboe, love torpedo, middle leg, bald-headed hermit, blue-veined custard chucker, chutney ferret and many more... There are, in fact, a total of 467 recognized terms, according to *Roger's Profanisaurus*, the authority in these matters. The title of this design comes from the classic movie *Young Frankenstein*.

Achieving monster erections is big business in more ways than one. Those who feel dwarfed when engaging in hand-to-gland combat can obtain a wide range of pumps, weights, creams, pills and other gadgets too painful to mention. In the end, you need to bear in mind the old adage "It's not the size, but what you do with it." Elementary study of sexual techniques and accurate location of the clitoris (see "Where's the Magic Bean?") are far more likely to turn on your partner than sporting a medically-enhanced monster with the size and appearance of a part-baked French loaf.

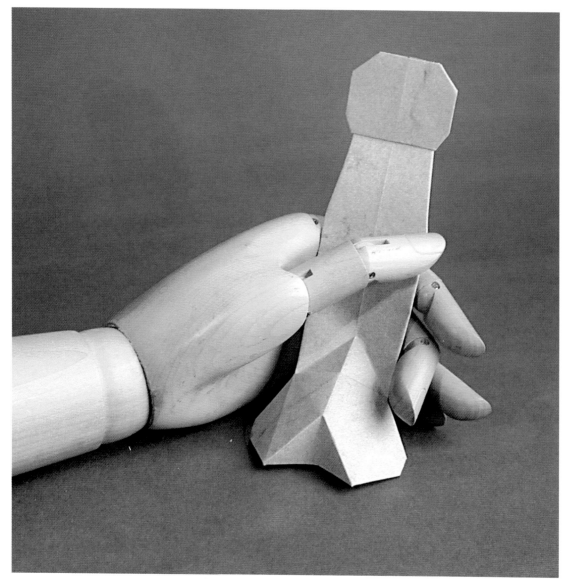

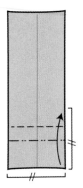

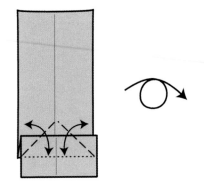

1. Start with half a sheet of A4, creased
   in half (or a dollar bill for a stubbier,
   more girthsome result). Pleat upwards
   a section to a point as high as the paper
   is wide.

2. Crease both corners at 45° to lie along
   the hidden edge underneath. Unfold.

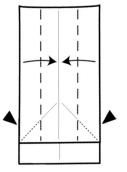

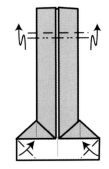

3. Fold either side of the upper section
   to the center crease. Flatten the hidden
   corners into neat triangles.

4. The two lower corners fold in.
   Make a pleat at the upper end,
   to form the "corona".

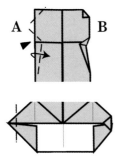

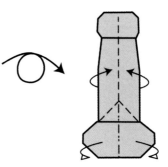

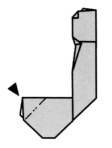

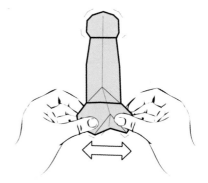

5. Round the lower sharp corners, then shape the head by folding two sides in and squashing the corners (**A**). The completed sides should resemble **B**.

6. Turn the paper over. Use the creases shown to fold the upper half together and the lower half away from you.

7. Like this. Push in the triangular section shown.

8. Here is the completed Schwanstucker. Hold by the balls and gently squeeze in and out for a realistic action.

Condomigami

Safe sex is more important than ever before, especially for models—origami models too. If your paper penis is starting to look a shade too creased, it may have contracted a social disease. The best approach is prevention: fold this simple paper protective and leave your cares behind.

Some historical facts: around 3000BC, King Minos of Crete made use of a fish bladder to prevent STDs. Similar objects were also known to be in use in Ancient Egypt, around 1000BC. Some historians claim that a "Dr. Condom" supplied Britain's King Charles II with sheaths to prevent illegitimate children. The name is most likely, however, to derive from the Latin *condon*, meaning "receptacle".

The Japanese are known to have used two types of condom—the "Kawagata", made of thin leather and the "Kabutogata", made from tortoiseshell. One can only imagine the marketing boys boasting about "increased sensitivity"... The legendary Casanova made regular use of a condom, which he referred to as his "English Riding Coat". Rubber condoms were first mass-produced around 1850, after Charles Goodyear developed the vulcanisation of rubber. These were superceded in the 1930s by the liquid latex variety still used today.

The first proper advertisement for condoms was seen in the *New York Times*, which published an advert for "Dr. Power's French Preventatives". The phrase "French letters" or more simply "Frenchies" has been used ever since. A more recent innovation is that of flavored condoms, though whether they were ever intended to be chewed is not too clear. The prospect of having a post-coital nibble and finding a "soft-center" doesn't bear thinking about…

The width of the paper should be $\frac{2}{3}$ x your circumference. The length of the paper should be $1\frac{1}{3}$ your "excited" length.

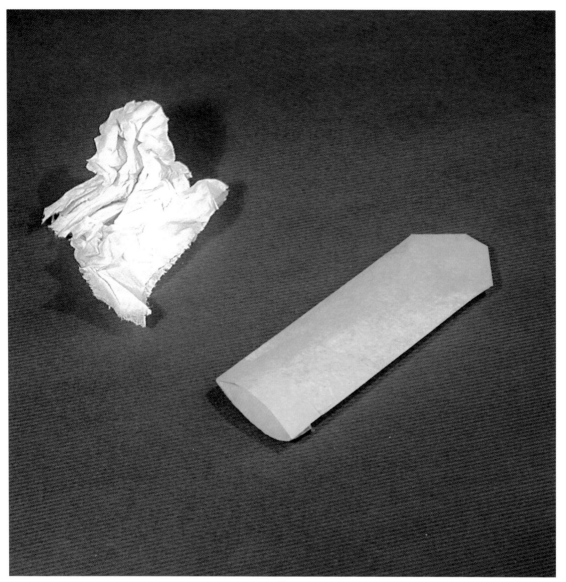

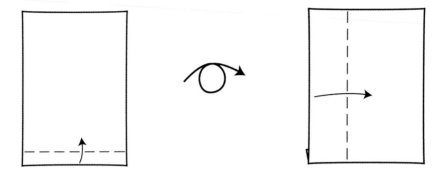

1. Start with a rectangle of paper (see formulae on page 20). Fold a small strip over at a short edge.

2. Fold the left-hand side over about a third of the way.

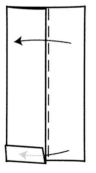

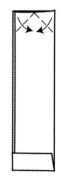

3. Fold the other side over as well, tucking into the pocket at the bottom.

4. Fold two corners at the top end to the center.

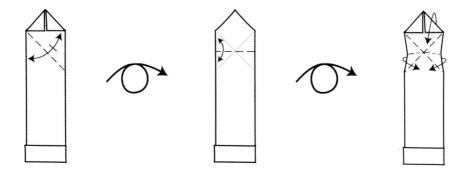

5. Like this. Now fold the top section over at 45°. Crease, unfold and repeat on the other side.

6. Turn the paper over. Fold the top of the X-shaped creases to touch the bottom, crease and unfold.

7. Use the creases shown to carefully collapse the paper downwards.

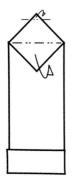

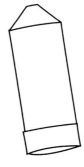

8. Tuck the triangular flap inside. Fold the tip behind for added comfort.

9. Ready to rock and roll!

Tradesman's Entrance

Bearing the Latin name *Gluteus maximus*, this part of the human anatomy could easily be mistaken for a character from Gladiator, but it's part of the body that holds endless fascination for men and women alike.

A massive 63% of women check out the backside first when assessing men's bodies— the majority seem to be in search of something called "buns of steel", although I'm not quite sure what advantage this would give you. Men are no less interested, although usually they are looking for buns of a somewhat softer nature. Indeed, there's a fan of "twin cheeks" for every devoted admirer of "twin peaks".

Considering the purely practical nature of the human backside (i.e. we sit on them) they play a leading role in human sexuality. The backside also plays an active part in sexual expression, for some straights and most gays, but we won't delve too deeply into the "snooker player's quandary" (deciding whether to pot the pink or the brown).

There are fewer alternative words for the backside than for the... ahem... front side. In English, the classic is "ass" or "arse", originally an Anglo-Saxon word. In some regions it is used as a generic term for the bottom of anything: e.g. "there's a slight crack on the arse end of that glass".

This particular design was inspired by a well-known Latin-American actress and singer who shall remain nameless to avoid legal action. However, if she feels slighted in any way, I'll be happy to compare this design with the real thing and make adjustments accordingly.

However, by carefully adjusting the locations of the creases or the shape of the initial sheet of paper, you can create your own ideal backside, wide, narrow, full, taut or simply huge. As an added bonus, by folding the creases between the legs in the final step, you can push the thighs together and cause the back to lower, presenting you with an perfect invitation to use the "tradesman's entrance".

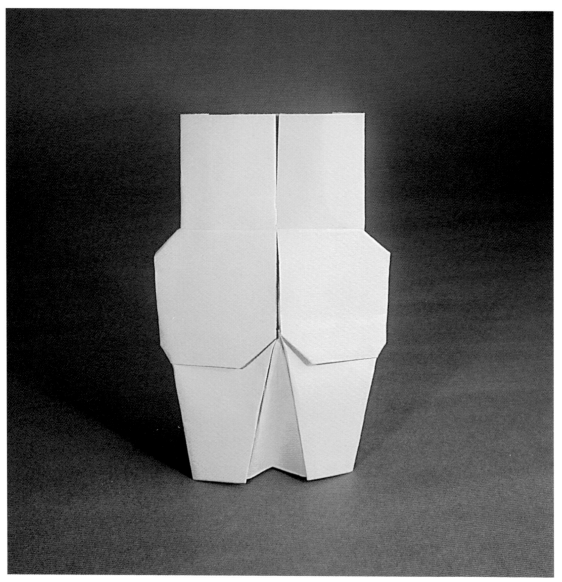

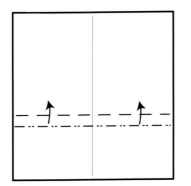

1. Start with a square, creased in half. Make a small pleat.

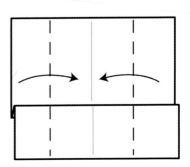

2. Fold the left and right edges into the center.

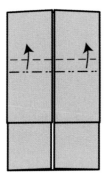

3. Make another small pleat.

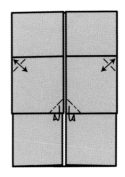

4. Fold the lower inside corners underneath. Crease the two upper outside corners.

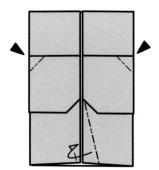

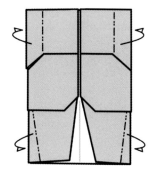

5. Shape the inside of the thighs by folding paper inside. Push the small triangular sections inside.

6. Fold the sides of the upper body behind. Shape the outside of the thighs.

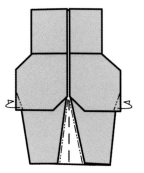

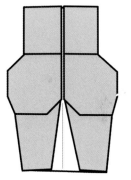

7. Shape the lower edges of the outer arse cheeks. Make an angled pleat along the inside of the thighs.

8. Here is the finished vision of delight.

Erupting Mount Fuji

Women have the fortunate ability to experience multiple orgasms during a sexual encounter, although this probably doesn't happen as often as they would like. The majority of men, on the other hand, manage just the one and pretty quickly at that. A whole industry has built up around prolonging an erection, with numerous creams, sprays, "energizing rings" and various other devices based around medieval instruments of torture.

The Kinsey Report (the most serious study of sexuality carried out in the U.S.) discovered that 6.4% of the young male population could achieve an erection within three seconds and reach orgasm in under ten! However, most of these would spend hours of single-handed practice, pushing their endurance onwards and upwards. Most men are able to "get there" in under 40 seconds and the lucky few reach the magical one minute barrier. This state of erectile nirvana is rare and precious, so girls, if you are lucky enough to land a "one minute wonder", never tell your friends or they'll be chasing after him as well.

Maintaining an erection without orgasm is also a variable factor. Young men can sustain a modest stiffy for several hours, but this ability lessens as middle age nears. Those interested in extending their endurance should look into Tantric Sex and pick up a few records by The Police. An alternative is to watch old episodes of Baywatch, though this can become a bone of contention.

And so to the moment known as the "gravy stroke". This is known somewhat more poetically as "le petit mort", since the moment of orgasm is apparently the closest we come to experiencing death. Men have their own unique brand of noises during orgasm, often known as the "sperm wail".

Working this action model requires a bit of practice. If nothing happens, look inside and make sure the creased edges are tight together and that the flaps of the smaller sheet are evenly spread—it is this friction which moves the "load" upwards. After a couple of trial runs, you'll be able to make your paper orgasms last for many seconds, thus impressing the ladies.

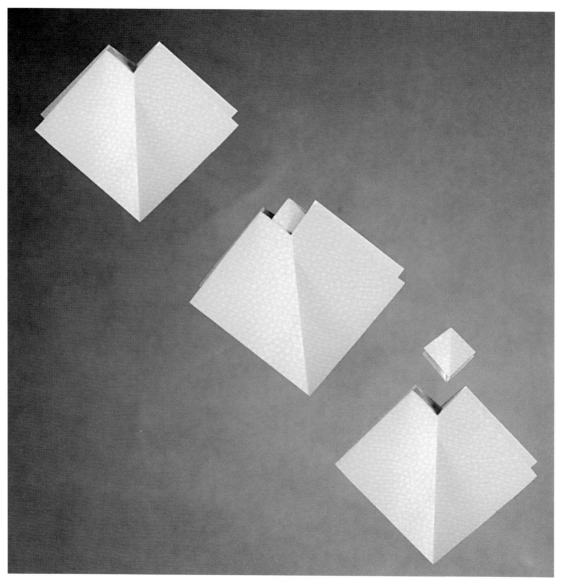

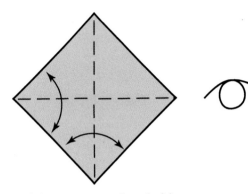 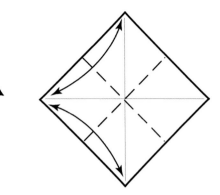

1. Start with a square, colored side towards you. Fold both diagonals.

2. Turn the paper over and fold in half both ways, side to side.

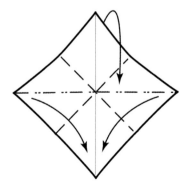 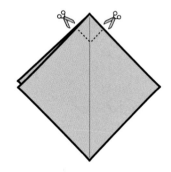

3. Use the creases shown to collapse the paper into a smaller square.

4. Carefully cut (or tear, if you must) a small square from the top corner of the paper. This was the original center of the square.

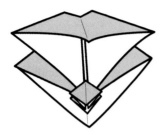

5. Slide the cut-off section inside the larger section, making sure each side is divided by a white double layer.

6. Keep sliding until it is half-way up.

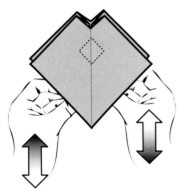

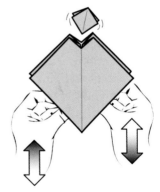

7. Hold the central white double layers, keeping the edges in the center tight together. Alternately move one hand towards you, the other away from you.

8. As you do this, the small sheet inside should climb up and eventually pop out of the gap at the top.

Bermuda Triangle

Most people know that the "Bermuda Triangle" is an area just off the south-eastern Atlantic coast of Florida, into which an unusually high number of ships, small boats, and aircraft have disappeared. It is also a euphemism for another warm, moist triangle into which things disappear, but of far greater interest to most men and gynaecologists.

The furry triangle in question has lots of names. While Innuit have 49 words for snow, the English-speaking population has many more words for this part of the anatomy! These include (skip to the next paragraph if easily offended) pussy, snatch, poochie, punanie, twat, mott box, cooter, coochie snorcher, cock socket and pink taco. For more suggestions, please go to see the essential *Vagina Monologues*.

The longest recorded female pubic hair reached the bearer's knees. Presumably it was neatly coiled away when a short skirt was worn. Normally though, pubic hairs have a genetic predisposition to stop growing at some point. Why should this be? Imagine the fun for hair-stylists if you could have your hair styled both above and below. A blow-dry would never be the same again.

It's also a fact that a lady's hair color doesn't always reflect the color "down below". Non-matching "collars and cuffs" is a perfectly normal state of affairs, and allows for some fun, armed with a small pair of scissors and selection of gentle colorants. You'd like green pubes? No problemo!

This design has entered into the pantheon of origami "classics", representing as it does a perfect marriage of art and technique, which is instantly recognizable, yet easy enough for any old idiot to fold. It allows you to test out any proposed pubic color combination by showing it to close friends and gauging their reactions. Simply choose paper that has skin color on one side and pube color on the other. By varying the amount of "lip" folded over, you can also compare the effect of a neatly trimmed triangle with a more luxuriant one.

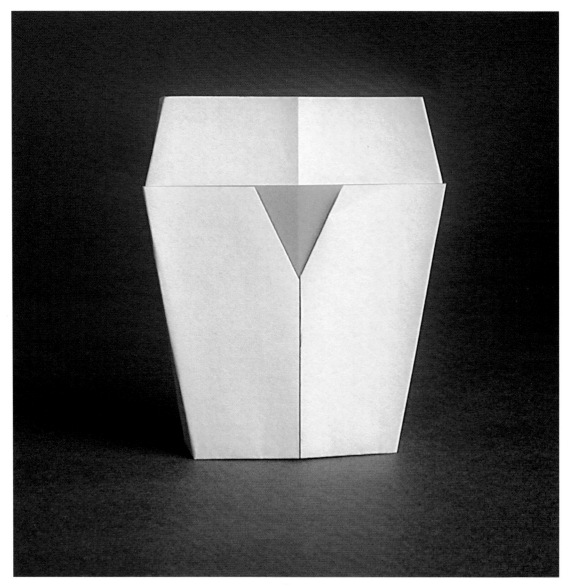

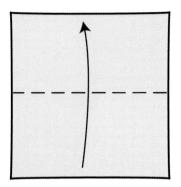

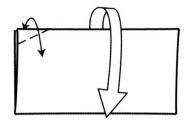

1. Start with a square, pubic color upwards. Fold in half from side to side.

2. Fold over two layers at a corner— check Step 4 for guidance as to how much. Open back out.

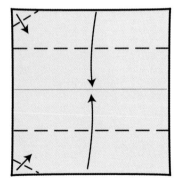

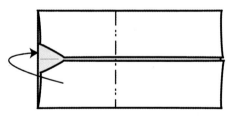

3. Fold in both corners, then fold each side to the center crease.

4. Fold the pubic section behind— see Step 5 for guidance.

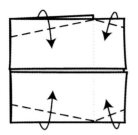 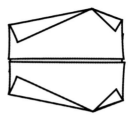

5. Shape the legs and hips with valley folds, to suit your tastes.

6. This is the result.

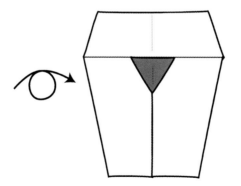

7. Turn over for the finished Bermuda Triangle.

A Glimpse of Paradise

It is generally agreed that an air of mystery is more likely to stoke up the sexual fires than having something shoved in your face. Indeed, the main point of most female fashion for the past 500 years has been to accentuate certain areas without giving too much away. Most sophisticated men prefer to be given gentle hints and subtle glimpses of the female form than to see the bland, airbrushed pin-ups pervading the pages of most men's magazines.

With film stars, much careful thought is given to the amount of flesh to bare. Men have no real problem, since we're not allowed to see stiffies on screen yet, so they just tone up their buns in the gym beforehand. That said, many leading men plan carefully if any pecker is likely to make it to the final cut. The standard practice is to nip backstage for a quick bit of "hand-to-gland massage", in order to ensure they are reasonably impressive, if not actually upstanding.

Women have a tougher decision. Do they go for a body double? Do they refuse the role? Or do they grin and bear it? The potential rewards can be impressive. A quick glimpse at Sharon Stone's film fee prior to and after her infamous "legs akimbo" scene in Basic Instinct provides clear evidence for this, especially when compared to Demi Moore's relentless quest to get her clothes off, and the speed at which the box office takings of her films have fallen. Many people agree that Marilyn Monroe's skirt billowing up was one of the sexiest sights of the 20th century.

Here's your chance to recreate a number of memorable scenes from Hollywood history, involving skirts. Be warned, however. It's not very easy to capture the grace of an elegant pair of legs using paper, so you'll need to keep practising this design. Use of "wet-folding" (damping the paper prior to folding) is advised. Feel free to alter proportions and angles until you have a satisfying result.

* Technical note: a shot of the female pubic region is known as a "beaver" shot, whereas a legs-open equivalent is known as a "split beaver" shot.

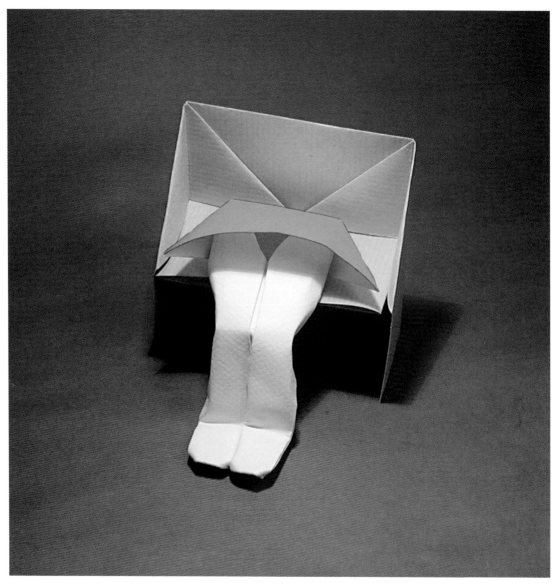

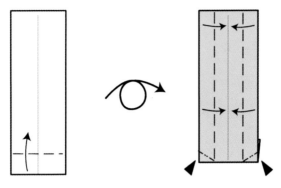

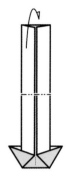

1. Start with a strip of paper about half the width of a sheet of A4. Crease in half. Fold up an amount just less than half the strip's width.

2. Turn the paper over and fold the long edges in to the center. Carefully squash at the base to form the skirt.

3. Fold the model in half behind.

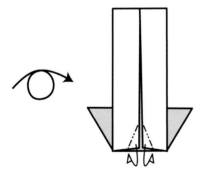

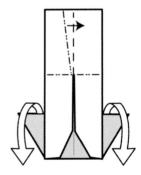

4. Turn the paper over. Fold two corners behind to form a suitably sized thatch.

5. Pull the skirt from behind. Make a pleat on the lower half of the legs, folding behind at the knees.

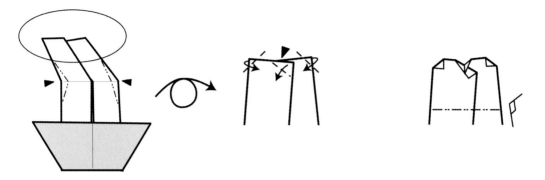

6. Like this. Shape the sides of the knees with gentle curved creases.

7. Here's the view beneath the feet. Fold the outside corners in, fold over and squash in the center.

8. This is the result. Fold the feet back at 90°.

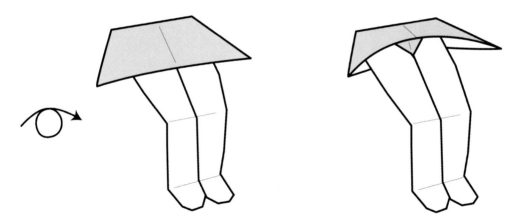

9. Turn over and adjust the posture. Wait for a gentle breeze.

Sperm

Whilst superficially resembling a tadpole, a sperm doesn't have anything like as long or as interesting a life. Technically speaking, a sperm is in fact the smallest cell in the body, little more than a mobile nucleus that tries to bring genetic material from the male parent to the egg of the female parent.

You may remember a popular beat combo from the '70s called 10cc. They were allegedly named after the amount ejaculated by a typical male. This is, in fact, incorrect: the average man only ejaculates 3cc (around 100 million sperm). Those of you worried about your own sperm-count can take a simple test to see if your sperm concentration meets the minimum requirement of 20 million sperm/ml as set by the World Health Organisation.

Even if you are "up to scratch", don't get too cocky. The average male pig ejaculate is approximately 3 liters. Another sexual Olympian is the honey possum, a tiny marsupial that lives on nectar and boasts the largest testes and sperm, in proportion to its body size, in the entire animal kingdom.

If you do decide to study your little tadpoles, you'll find most men have all the necessary equipment ready to hand. You'll need to learn about terms such as morphology (the shape of sperm), motility (the movement of sperm) and agglutination (the clumping of sperm). You'll have to be quick though, since the human sperm has only about 5 minutes in which to travel 7 inches at a rate of 0.0099 mph, before one of them strikes gold and the other 99,999,999 or so shuffle off their mortal coil.

Low sperm-counts are not always due to hereditary reasons; riding a bike for long periods of time, for example, can raise the temperature of the scrotum and affect sperm quality. If this concerns you, always take an adequate supply of ice cubes with which to line your cycling shorts.

Finally, if you feel the calling to donate, a sperm donor boom is apparently gathering steam in Denmark, where healthy young men (up to 80% of whom are students) can earn up to 34 Euros for a few minutes' enjoyable work!

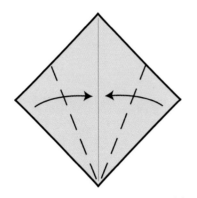

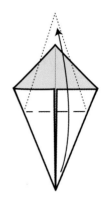

1. Start with a square of paper, white side underneath, with a creased diagonal. Fold two sides in to lie along the diagonal crease.

2. Fold the lower corner of the kite shape just past the upper corner.

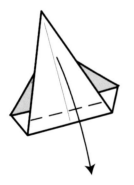

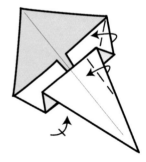

3. Leave a small gap and fold the point back down again.

4. Fold the side of the tail in at the body end. Part of the body paper folds in with it. Repeat on the other side.

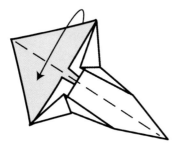

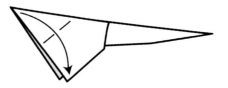

5. Fold the paper in half using the original diagonal.

6. Fold the top-left corner to meet the bottom corner.

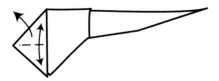

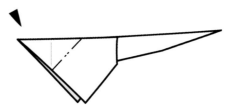

7. Fold the triangular flap in half, crease and unfold. Then unfold Step 6.

8. Reverse fold the point inside.

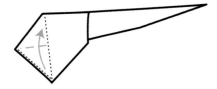

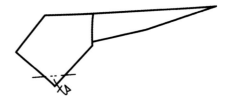

9. Refold the crease made in Step 7, locking the paper together.

10. Round the base of the body on both sides of the model.

11. The completed sperm. Now repeat 100 million times.

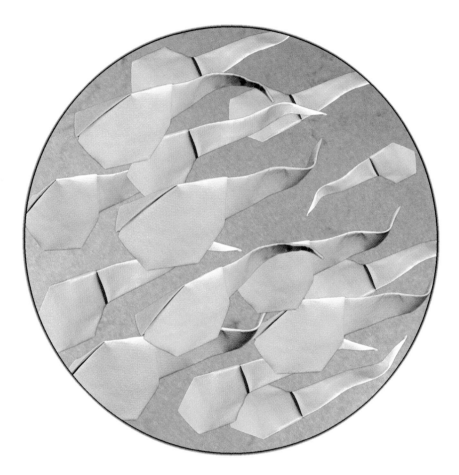

Sperm cells (mag. 3500x).

Boobs

Of all the female physical attributes that men have admired across the centuries, none can rival the breast. Actually, "admired" is too casual a word—"worshipped" might be nearer the mark. In ancient times, males and females were happy to wander about topless, but the advent of Christianity demanded women become more modest about their superstructure. By the Renaissance, larger breasts were considered most desirable, as can be seen in the acres of cleavage in paintings from that era. The Victorians set back boob-worship for many years, as they forced them into tight corsets and generally covered up about as much flesh as was humanly possible.

An important turning point was the growth of the movie industry. Stars such as Marilyn Monroe, Jane Russell and Diana Dors made a well-filled jumper the first thing many young men looked for in a woman. In Great Britain, however, the delights of the naked breast were still confined to the top shelf of newsagents until the tabloids came up with the concept of the Page 3 Girl. Finally, workmen of all persuasions could enjoy their morning "cuppa" whilst learning that "lovely Linda, 18, wants to be an air hostess". The female liberation movement furthered their aims by burning bras, a sentiment which had overwhelming support from most males. Nowadays, we're quite used to seeing boobs, but they still have the capability to shock, if exposed in unlikely situations. The paparazzi will still go to the most extraordinary lengths in order to catch the slightest glimpse of a major celebrity's boob or nipple.

One of the enduring fascinations of breasts is the huge range of shapes and sizes. The phallus, for all the variations in length and girth, is dull by comparison! Yes folks, there are large ones, small ones, pointy ones, squashy ones, firm ones and much more besides. As if this weren't enough, each boob is equipped with a nipple. These too come in a wide range of shapes and sizes, and are surrounded by areolae—the word that few men can spell, let alone pronounce properly.

The attention devoted to boobs is probably a sign of just how far we have to travel along the road towards true civilisation. Instead of valuing people's minds and abilities, the typical male of species is still more impressed by a particularly large pair of breasts.

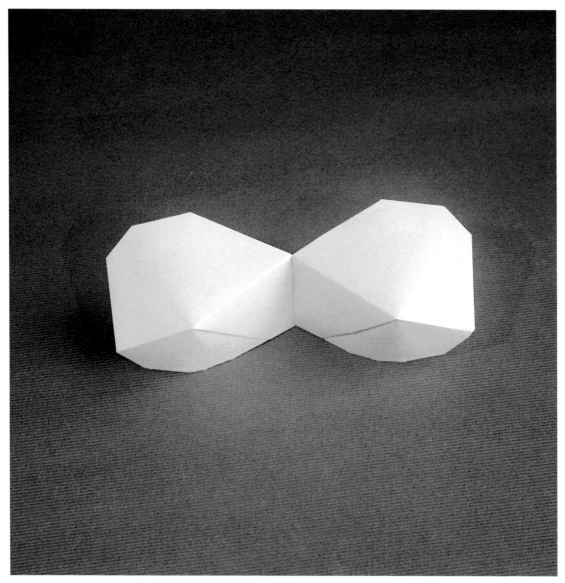

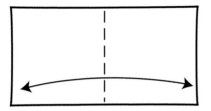 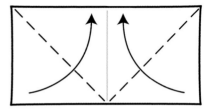

1. Start with a 2 x 1 rectangle. Fold in half from right to left, crease and unfold.

2. Fold both lower halves to the vertical crease.

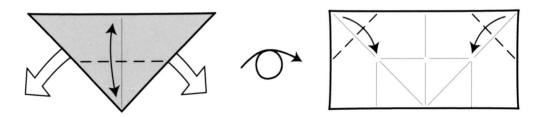

3. Turn the paper over, fold the lower point to the top, crease and unfold. Unfold back to Step 1.

4. Turn the paper over, then fold the two corners in to meet the intersection of the creases.

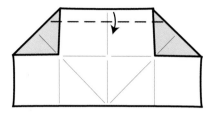

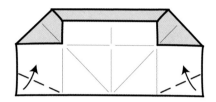

5. Fold over about one third of the top section.

6. Fold the lower corners over so that their inside edges point towards the colored corner (see dotted line on the next diagram).

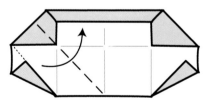

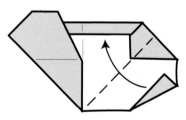

7. Refold the left-hand side on the existing crease.

8. Refold the right-hand side as in Step 7.

9. This is the result. Turn the paper over.

10. (Enlarged view.) Fold two matching corners over.

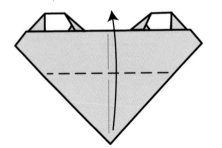

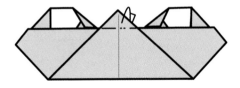

11. Refold on an existing crease.

12. Fold the tip of the point over the folded edge.

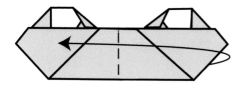
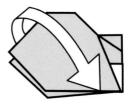

13. Fold the whole model in half.

14. Open and lovingly shape the paper.

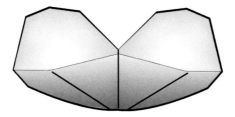

15. The completed pair.

Coupling

As a growing youngster, I was always fascinated by the myriad positional possibilities of sexual congress. I knew that it could be performed in other positions than just face to face, but it came as a real shock to discover it was possible from behind! I thought long and hard about the mechanics of the act and the possible pain involved for either or both parties. As an author in the late summer of his years, I've been lucky enough to try both alternatives and a couple of others besides. However, even during my years as a rock star, the chances of being involved in regular, gratuitous sex, let alone serious and hygienic group sex came far too infrequently.

The Romans were perhaps the first culture to take group-sex seriously. No self-respecting Senator would consider holding a swingers' party without an orgy. Caterers would be required to supply not only large quantities of *Pullum frontonianum* (chicken wings) and red wine but also sufficient vestal virgins and variously colored and acrobatic courtesans to satisfy the refined and inventive whims of his guests. I'd imagine it's pretty similar if you attend private parties hosted by top ranking Major League stars. For an insight into these heady days, please catch a few minutes' worth of the movie *Caligula*.

Anyone serious about positional play should invest in an illustrated edition of the Kama Sutra. This epic work covers such intriguing positions as "the sporting of a sparrow", "the churning of the cream" and "the splitting of the bamboo". You are even offered basic guidance on methods of penis enlargement: "First rub your penis with wasp stings and massage it with sweet oil. When it swells, let it dangle for ten nights through a hole in your bed."

Woody Allen once said, "Sex between two people is a beautiful thing; between five it's fantastic!" I'm sure he's right and by folding lots of examples of this design, you can create an elaborate group-sex-scene with as many partners as you like, then try to persuade your friends to re-enact it after a night of heavy drinking.

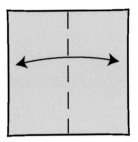

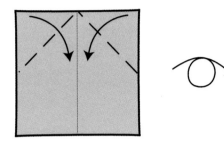

1. **Start with a square, colored side up. Fold in half, crease and unfold.**

2. **Fold two corners to meet the center.**

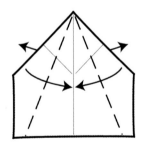

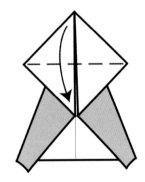

3. **Turn the paper over, then take the folded edges to the center crease, allowing the flaps to pop out from underneath.**

4. **Fold the top square in half.**

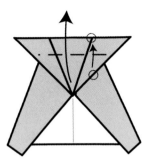

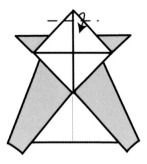

5. Fold part of the same flap back upwards, so the circled areas meet.

6. Fold the tip of the head back over.

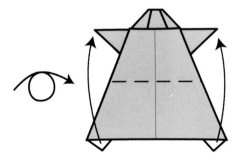

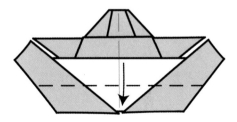

7. Turn the paper over again, then fold the lower corners to meet the tips of the arms.

8. Fold the white triangular section down (in half).

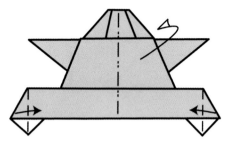

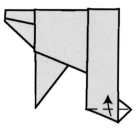

9. Fold the whole body in half underneath.

10. Narrow the feet by folding them in half.

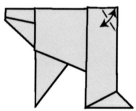

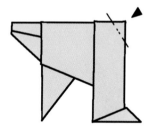

11. Fold part of the backside over, crease and unfold.

12. Now tenderly push in the triangle of paper over the nether regions. Experienced paperfolders might try forming a closed sink.

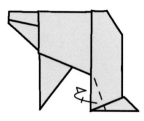

13. Narrow the front of each leg.

14. Ready for action!

The Chain Gang.

The Human Pyramid.

The Spit-roast.

Subtle Ploy

Few items of furniture play a more important part in our lives than the bed—perhaps only the toilet and the back-scrubber. Most of us were conceived in bed, many of us only ever make love in one, and we spend nearly a third of our lives in them! Sleeping Beauty allegedly spent 100 years in one, Goldilocks liked beds with that great smell of bear, John & Yoko famously made a "bed-in" protest. Most sit-coms can't manage an entire episode without some combination of the leading actors being seen in bed together.

This design has many notable features. Most importantly, it can be used to store and carry a condom around, while keeping it in prime condition. Also, it is both an example of "pureland" origami (where only simple valley and mountain creases are used), and "climactic origami", where the finished design is only revealed at the very last step. As if this wasn't enough, the design is perfect for attempted seduction.

When you've spent a few hours in the company of someone you find attractive and feel the time is right to take things a step further, how best should you raise the subject of nookie? Lame stories about coming in for a cup of coffee or to see your interesting collection of etchings are unlikely to impress. I once had a friend called Tim who hailed from Alabama. He checked out the lie of the land with the charming phrase, "Wanna fuck?" Whilst not yielding a high success rate, it did save a lot of time, effort and wasted small-talk for both parties.

Naughty Origamians have a more sophisticated option. Fold this bed from a square four times as wide as your condom (you do use condoms, don't you?) then slide the packet into the underside of the bed. There it can reside, safe and sound for several weeks, dependant on your charm. When the moment of truth arrives, unfold and with practiced fingers shape the bed, then drop the condom on top of it. Push the message of love across the table to your partner and flash your sexiest smile.

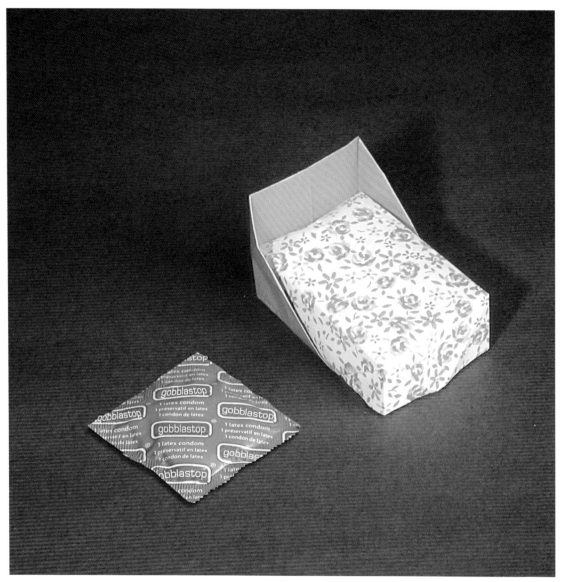

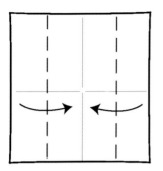

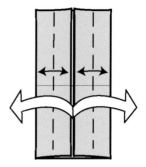

1. Start with a square creased in half both ways. Fold two opposite sides to the center.

2. Fold each side in half again, crease firmly, then unfold back to the square.

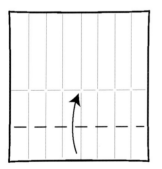

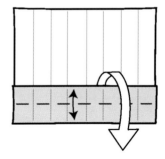

3. Fold a side to the center.

4. Fold this section in half again, then unfold completely.

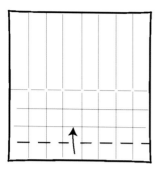

5. Off we go then. Fold in an eighth section of paper.

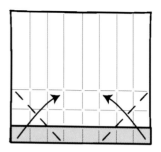

6. Fold in two corners starting 3 eighths in.

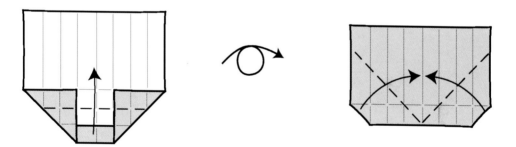

7. Fold over a quarter section.

8. Turn the paper over, fold each half of the long folded edge to meet the center.

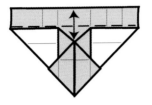

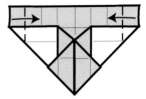

9. Fold over the top eighth, crease and unfold.

10. Fold in the outer eighth sections.

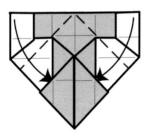

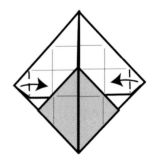

11. Fold each half of the upper edge to meet the center, tucking them into the small pockets.

12. Fold over the outside sections of the triangles.

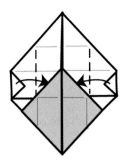

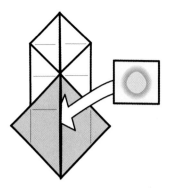

13. Next fold over again, using existing creases. Carefully tuck these layers into the pockets.

14. At this stage you can pop the prophylactic inside the pocket.

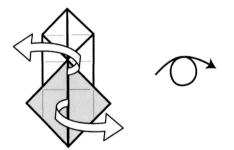

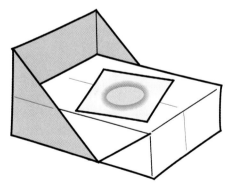

15. Open the layers and shape the corners of the bed. (I'd do this once or twice in advance to have it quickly open into shape.)

16. The completed bed, all primed and ready for hot action.

Where's the Magic Bean?

Over the past 50 years there has been a huge increase in the time at school devoted to sexual biology. However, we still seem to feel that the giving of sexual pleasure is an unsuitable subject for the classroom. It would probably be a difficult topic to ease smoothly into the curriculum.

And so, the end result is that there are still one or two men who don't know a) the position and b) the function of the clitoris. First let's tackle the easier of the two: the function. The clitoris is present solely to provide its lucky owner with sexual pleasure, and it is the only organ in either male or female bodies with pleasure as its sole job.

Location, however, is a bit more of a mystery. Most men know "more or less" where it is, but if persuaded to play a clitoral version of "pin the tail on the donkey", few would win first prize. If there were a word for the game in the dictionary, it would be probably be "frigmarole". Now as the sexually-educated readers that you undoubtedly are, you won't need any guidance on the subject, but you may have a "friend" who does!

Female readers will know from weary experience that many men who can happily track their way through jungles and across deserts with no more than a compass and Swiss Army knife, still need an endless stream of "Up a bit... Left a bit... Stop!" type instructions when hunting the magic bean. However, your problems are now at an end. Naughty Origami has the perfect solution to your problems: free, easy to use, eminently practical and disposable...

Depending on your terrain, you may need to experiment with the starting size of paper, but once you've found the correct measurement, be sure to keep suitable sheets of pre-creased paper in your purse at all times. Whilst he's fumbling with his boxer shorts, quickly fold and (carefully) insert your paper helper. Lie back and await the pleasures to come. If the light is dimmed, you could use fluorescent paper. And men, if all else fails, swallow your pride and simply *ask* where it is!

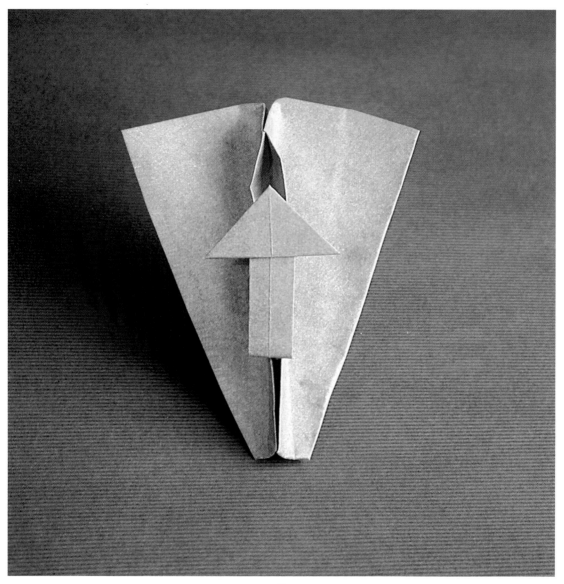

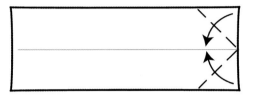

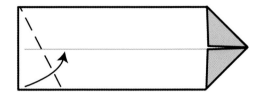

1. Start with a dollar bill, or any piece of paper about this size. Fold the long sides together, crease and unfold. At the right-hand end, fold both corners to the center.

2. At the left-hand end, fold the lower corner to meet the center crease; the other end of the crease is the top-left corner.

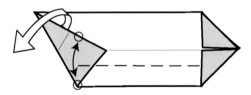

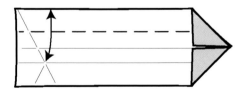

3. Fold the lower corner of the colored triangle (on the left), so that it touches the top edge of the same flap. Crease and unfold. (The crease shouldn't extend into the triangles on the right.)

4. Fold the top edge down to meet the crease you've just made, crease and unfold. This cunningly divides the height into three.

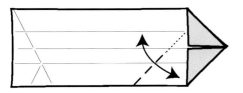

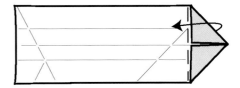

5. Starting at the upper one third crease, fold the lower corner of the colored triangle to meet the center, crease the lower part of the crease only, then unfold.

6. Fold over the colored triangle.

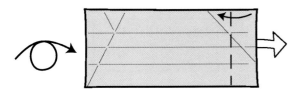

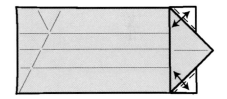

7. Turn the paper over. Fold the right-hand edge to meet the crease made in Step 6, allowing the tip of the arrow-head to pop out from underneath.

8. Fold the small white triangles over, crease and unfold.

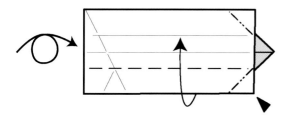 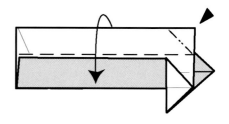

9. Turn the paper over. Fold over the lower third, carefully flattening the triangle as you do so.

10. Repeat on the opposite side.

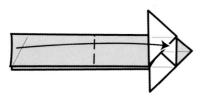 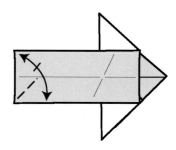

11. Fold the left-hand edge to meet the edges of the arrow-head.

12. Fold upper and lower edges over to meet the left-hand edge, creasing only to the center.

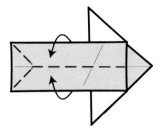

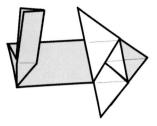

13. Fold all three creases shown at the same time. The flap will narrow and stick out at right-angles to the rest of the paper.

14. Like this. Trim off the end of this narrow flap if necessary.

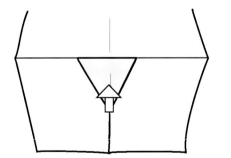

15. Your route-map to pleasure is now complete.

Randy Rabbits

We often look to the animal kingdom for inspiration when describing our own behaviour. "At it like rabbits" is a well-known phrase and also well-chosen. If you put a pair of fertile rabbits on an island with plenty of food and no predators, within a year you'll have 6 million of the furry devils to contend with.

Evidence for this lies in records of the latter part of the 18th century when rabbits were introduced to Australia to supplement the settlers' diets. Within a few years, rabbit numbers reached mammoth proportions. As a fun project, you might care to replicate the great Australian plague yourself. Simply buy several thousand sheets of brown paper in assorted sizes, then fold each one into a rabbit.

As a lover, the typical male rabbit is somewhat lacking in the department of amatory skills. Although endowed with a hip action that a porn star would be proud of, they are selfish beasts. The average length of rabbit rumpy-pumpy is around 8 seconds, followed by precious little pillow-talk. So if your partner complains that you are a "one-minute wonder", point out that in the rabbit fraternity, you'd be in the top ten!

The hare, on the other hand, puts far more effort into his love-making. After each copulation, they fall on their sides in a kind of epileptic fit, showing the whites of the eyes and salivating. The animal then has spasmodic twitches, and lies panting for several moments until the nervous system recovers.

Once you've folded one rabbit, it wouldn't be fair to not provide a partner. Why not fold lots of these furry critters and leave them "in action" in the most inappropriate places: on your boss's desk, on the top of condom machines, in department store windows... Use your imagination—I'm sure you'll think of somewhere!

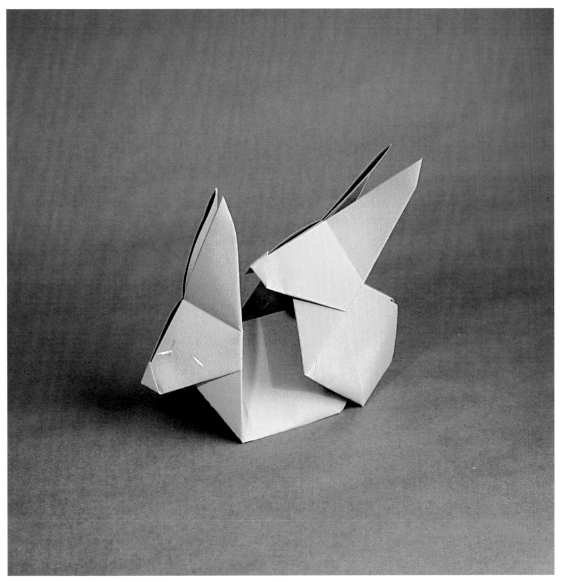

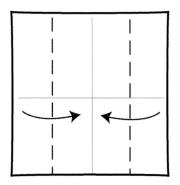

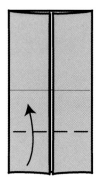

1. Start with a square, creased in half both ways. Fold left and right sides in to the center.

2. Fold the lower short edge to the center.

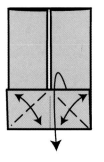

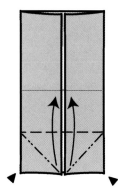

3. Fold the outer short edges to the lower edge, crease and unfold. Unfold back to Step 2.

4. Use the crease shown to lift the first layers of paper and squash upwards into triangular flaps.

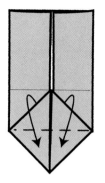

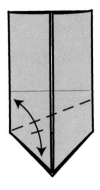

5. Fold both triangular flaps down.

6. Fold the lower-left edge to the vertical left-hand edge. Crease and unfold, then repeat on the other side.

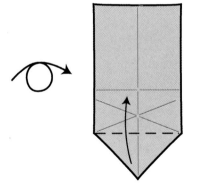

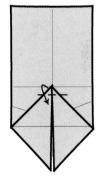

7. Turn the paper over. Fold the upper triangular flap over.

8. Fold over a small point to form the nose.

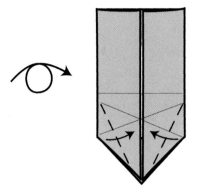

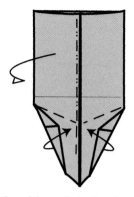

9. Turn the paper over again. Fold the ears over (see next drawing).

10. Fold the sides of the body away from you, at the same time swing the ears together and over the top of the body. Not as difficult as it sounds!

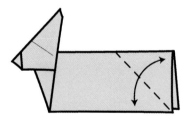

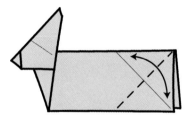

11. Fold the rear edge to meet the lower edge, crease and unfold.

12. Repeat the last move, folding the short edge upwards.

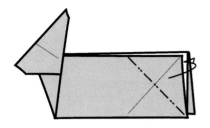

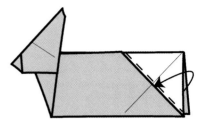

13. Fold the first layer of paper inside the layers.

14. Now fold the remaining layers inside as well.

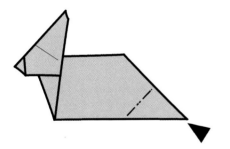

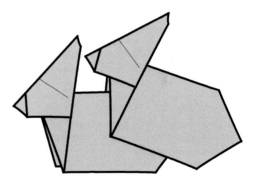

15. Carefully push the point inside, using an existing crease.

16. Your rabbit is complete. Fold it a partner as soon as possible!

Going Down

The tongue has a busy life. Not only is it required to speak at least one language, it must be capable of separating sweet from sour and salt from bitter; it needs the ability to blow raspberries; and last, but definitely not least, it can be an instrument for giving pleasure to one's partner. Over the centuries a rich folklore has developed around the tongue. Did you know the following?

- It's impossible to lick your elbow?

- A crocodile can't stick its tongue out, however rude it is.

- Your tongue has a unique pattern, like a fingerprint.

- Three out of four readers will by now have tried to lick their elbow.

Artists as varied as Jeff Beck, Deep Purple, Freddie King and Linkin Park have sung a song called "Going Down", and they don't just mean the charts. Shania Twain, on the other hand, bucked the trend by singing, "I ain't going down".

The oral pleasuring of your partner can also play a part in sexual politics. During the T'ang Dynasty, the Empress Wu-Hu passed a special law regarding oral sex. She felt that by pleasuring a man, the woman was acknowledging male supremacy. She therefore insisted that all visiting dignitaries should show their respect to her by orally pleasuring her upon their meeting. She would throw open her robe and her guest would "go on down".

This model can be used to stimulate almost any part of the body, providing you are allowed access to it and are sufficiently flexible to reach it. With practice you'll soon become a keen, cunning linguist, and don't forget, oral sex makes your day, but anal sex makes your hole weak.

As ever, we can look to the bible for a final comment. Proverbs 15:4 says: "A wholesome tongue is a tree of life, but perverseness in it breaks the spirit." A fine philosophy by which to live your life.

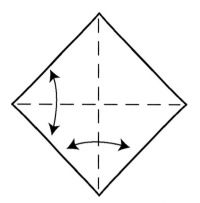

1. Start with a square, white side upwards. Crease both diagonals.

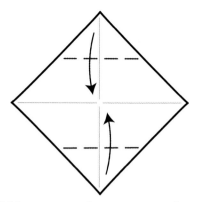

2. Fold two opposite corners to the center.

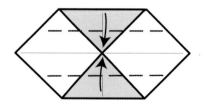

3. Then fold both flaps in half again.

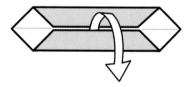

4. Fully unfold the lower edge, then turn the paper over.

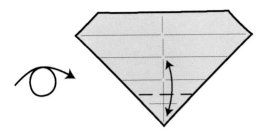

5. Fold the lower corner to meet the third horizontal crease.

6. Turn over and make a pleat.

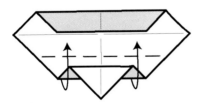

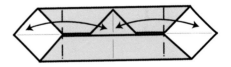

7. Valley fold the lower section upwards.

8. Fold left and right corners to the center, crease and unfold.

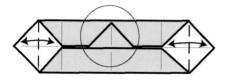

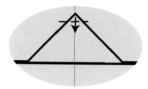

9. Fold the small squares (left and right) in half, then unfold. Next, look at the central flap.

10. Fold down the top corner of the triangular flap.

11. Now carefully add these two creases.

12. To help the action, emphasize the central valley crease.

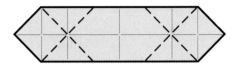

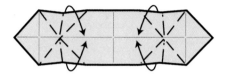

13. Turn the paper over and add these 45° creases at either end.

14. Use the recent creases to carefully collapse the paper towards the center.

15. Like this. Tuck the inside flaps underneath into pockets. Turn the paper back over.

16. Fold the tongue out on creases made in Steps 11 and 12. To operate, flex the sides backwards, then relax the paper. Practise to develop a smooth action!

French Tickler

The French Tickler, which is also known as Goat's Eyelid or Happy Ring, was reputedly first made by Tibetan lamas in the 13th century. It was made from the eyelids and eyelashes of a slaughtered goat. When this delightful object was tied around the penis, the eyelashes provided a lucky lady with a pleasant tickling sensation. (In response to many complaints by vegetarians, more modern versions are made from plastic.)

Erotic toys go back as far as Ancient Babylon, where sculptures, unmistakably in the form of a dildo (or a regular type of carrot) have been discovered. Erotic toys are even mentioned in the Bible. Ezekiel 16:17 offers: "Thou hast also taken thy fair jewels of my gold and silver and madest to thyself images of men, and didst commit whoredom with them." A nice turn of phrase indeed.

The main problem with many commercial "love aids" is that they are more likely to inspire howls of laughter rather than stimulate raging (or flagging) libidos. Displaying your crown jewels in a furry blue pouch may keep them warm, but sexy? I suspect not. Then there's the problem of fitting/using them properly. To avoid embarrassment, make sure you read the instructions carefully and go through a few dry runs before impressing your partner. Where appropriate, keep a good supply of batteries lying in a handy location—mains transformers are really not a good idea.

This item of Naughty Origami should be folded from a sheet of paper that results in a suitably-sized hole. After an initial (private) survey, I can reveal that a half a sheet of A4 paper seems to suit most men. Lucky gentleman can then boast of their A4s. Women can hand one over, folded from A3, with the tantalizing offer, "If you fit this, you're in luck."

Mathematically-inclined folders can work out the optimum-sized paper with this formula:

$$L \times \tfrac{3}{4} = C^{\text{dick}}$$

L = *length of the longest side of the rectangle*
C = *circumference of your pink clarinet*

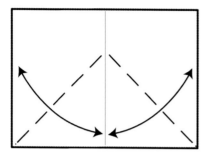

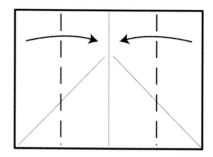

1. Start with a sheet of A5 (half an A4) or similar rectangle, creased in half. Fold both outer edges to the lower edge, crease and unfold.

2. Fold both outer edges to the center.

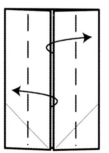

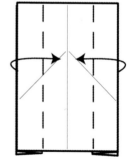

3. Fold single layers back out again.

4. Turn the paper over and fold both edges to the center.

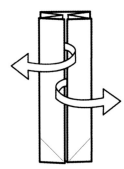

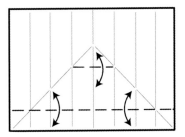

5. Unfold back to Step 1.

6. Add valley creases where shown.

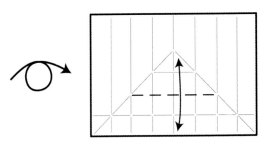

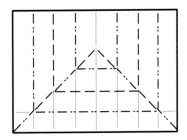

7. Turn the paper over and add the half-way crease.

8. Emphasize the creases shown. Most are correct, but you may need to alter some from valley to mountain etc.

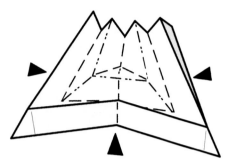

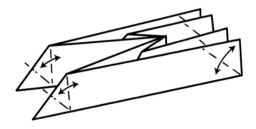

9. Here's the fold in progress. Keep flattening the paper.

10. Add the creases shown, two at each of the left-hand edges, four on the right-hand edges.

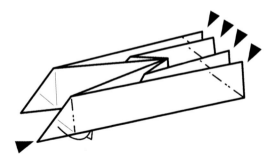

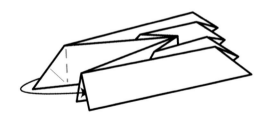

11. Push all four corners inside on the right, and the nearest corner only on the left.

12. Tuck the rear left-hand point inside the other pocket.

13. Fold over the flap inside using the crease made in Step 10. This is easier if you lift up the outer edge.

14. Carefully open out the paper and shape it into a circle, swinging the "ticklers" left and right to help.

15. Complete.

Memphis Bell

This design was named in honor of the "Memphis Belle", one of the first B-17s to complete 25 combat missions in World War II, whose exploits have entered into legendary status and even been the subject of a Hollywood film. This particular paper tribute aircraft is unlikely to survive 25 missions, although it's just about possible. It is also inherently unstable in flight, due the center of gravity being too far forward, but if you added a 30-foot steel penis to the front of a Lear jet, it would be unstable too. I know because I tried it.

When launching a paper airplane, you should consider three things: the speed of launch, the angle at which you launch it, and the angle of the wings (known as "dihedral", aviation fans). All three will affect each other. You need to concentrate on one factor—for example, alter the dihedral, then launch it and see how it affects the flight. Keep altering until you have the perfect angle. Then work on the speed of launch. True paper aviators can spend several hours determining the "best" launch method, while their partners look on in rapt amazement.

Having mastered the launch technique, there are a number of thrilling games you can play with your friends, using this design, such as:

• Who can make the longest flight? In the tradition of golf, if you see it hurtling towards anyone, you should shout out, "Foreskin!"

• Who can achieve the longest time in the air? This is best achieved by launching from the top of a skyscraper.

• Who can make the plane land in a beer? Please do ensure the beer belongs to a mate, not the large skinhead in the corner.

• Who can make the plane land in the cleavage of a likely target? This requires serious levels of concentration, a steady hand and an almost impossible degree of good fortune.

The more adventurous may even try to achieve actual penetration from 3 feet away. Ensure your partner is a) ready and b) quite excited! In all cases, use suitable paper. It needs to be firm, yet gentle, stiff, yet yielding.

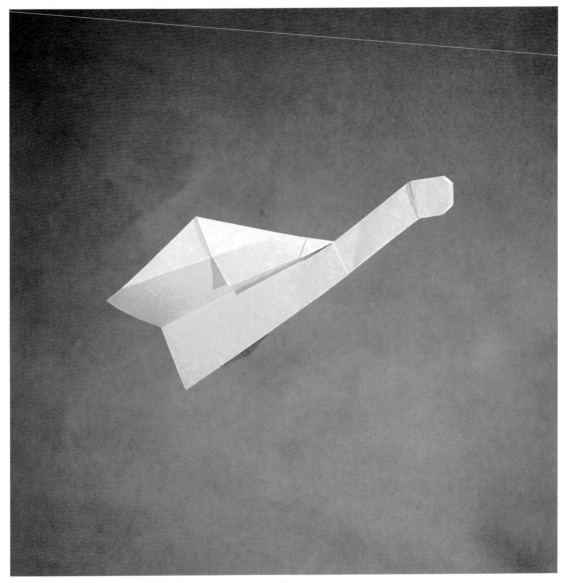

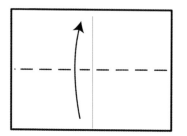

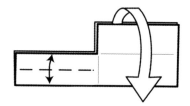

1. Start with an A4 or similar rectangle, creased in half between the short edges. Fold the long edges together.

2. Fold the long edges together, crease and unfold.

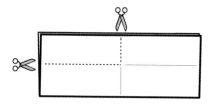

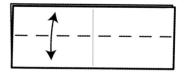

3. Cut or (carefully) tear the top-left quarter out.

4. Crease the left section in half, then open the paper out.

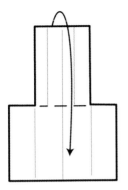

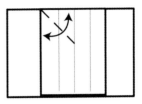

5. Rotate to this position and fold the top edge down in half.

6. Make a 45° crease on the left-hand side.

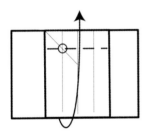

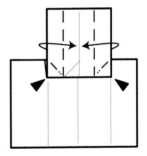

7. Fold the central flap back upwards, using the circled point as a reference.

8. Fold the sides of the narrow flap to the center, carefully flattening the inside corners into triangles. (see next picture).

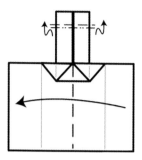

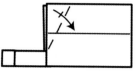

9. Make a small pleat at the bell end of the paper, then fold the paper in half.

10. Fold the top-left corner of the wings down to meet the horizontal crease.

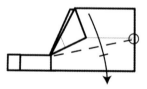

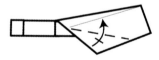

11. Fold the wings over again—note where the crease ends.

12. Then fold the leading edge back to meet the crease (on both sides).

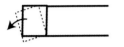 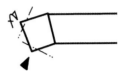

13. Pull the bell section forwards and downwards.

14. Finally, fold in the top corners and reverse fold the bottom corner to round off the end.

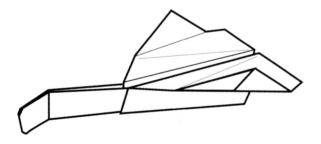

15. Open the main part of the wings horizontally and adjust the front flaps slightly upwards. Launch slowly at a slight upwards angle.

Bibliography & Credits

Kokigami – Performance Enhancing Adornments for the Adventurous Man, Burton Silver & Heather Busch (1992)

A Revised History of Kokigami, John Thomas (1945)

Pornigami, Master Sugoi (1994)

The Lonely Man II (The Second Coming), Alasdair Post-Quinn (1923)

Japanese Erotic Origami, Kunihara Kasahiko (1966)

The Origins of the Paper Penis, Bronco Sinkin (private publication, 1972)

Sexual Origami and Architecture, Klee et al, Bauhaus archives (1935)

Poontang with Paper, Lord Brill of Worth Hall (1923)

One Thousand Years of Japanese Erotic Arts 650–1650, N'Gobola Wushi (1979)

Teach Yourself Aeronautics, Manfred von Richthofen

Super Kinky Origami Animals, Nick Robinson (2000)

Rabbits, Hares and Hamsters, Silke Schroeder (1963)

Roger's Profanisaurus, Viz (2002)

Dedicated to Thoki Yenn, who would have loved this book had he lived to read it.

Thanks must go to the following: fellow Naughty Origamists Bronco Sinkin, Zack Brown, Alasdair Post-Quinn, Master Sugoi, Mark Leonard (Tradesman's Entrance), Kunihiko Kasahara (Mons), Marc Kirschenbaum (Coupling), and Mark Kennedy; Mark Robinson (no relation), who carefully folded everything without excitement, looking for errors; Gareth and Rosemary from New Holland; my wife Alison, daughter Daisy ("Dad, you're so not cool") and son Nick; Gomez and Morticia Cat; Mick, Joe and Warren; about 18 stick insects; any paper-folders out there with a sense of humor; the Sheffield United Soccer Squad; David and Stan Mead, still dreaming away those miles; the Mohul and Dilshad Curry Houses; Love Hearts; Pifco products; all at Hurst House; all members of Poppadom (see www.poppadom.org.uk).

If you want to try some more complex Naughty Origami, have a look around www.underground.zork.net.

First published in the United States
of America in 2004 by
UNIVERSE PUBLISHING
A division of Rizzoli International
Publications, Inc.
300 Park Avenue South
New York, NY 10010
www.rizzoliusa.com

First published in the UK as *Adult Origami* in
2004 by New Holland Publishers (UK) Ltd
www.newhollandpublishers.com

10 9 8 7 6 5 4 3 2

Second printing

ISBN: 0–7893–1207–7
Library of Congress Catalog Control
Number: 2004102977

Editor: Gareth Jones
Editorial Direction: Rosemary Wilkinson
Photography: Nick Robinson
Artwork: Nick Robinson
Design: Paul Wright @ Cube
Cover Design: Gloria Ahn

Reproduction by
Modern Age Repro, Hong Kong
Printed and bound by
Craft Print International, Singapore